Anthropocene Lullaby

Books by K. A. Hays

Dear Apocalypse
Early Creatures, Native Gods
Windthrow
Anthropocene Lullaby

Anthropocene Lullaby

◉

K. A. Hays

Carnegie Mellon University Press
Pittsburgh 2022

Acknowledgments

I would like to thank the editors of the following journals, in which these poems have appeared, some in altered form or under different titles:

Agni: "Lines written at Dog's Head Falls, Johnson, Vermont"; *American Literary Review*: "It's not for me but I'm here in it"; *Bennington Review*: "From my pocket on a hike, a tone warns me," "Lines written in the Down East Community Hospital emergency room, Machias, Maine"; *Cream City Review*: "As after a hatch tadpoles heat the bank"; *Diode Poetry Journal*: "Walking with Zoe, holding a bag of her warm shit"; *Gettysburg Review*: "I'm finefinefine & pleased," "Anthropocene Sonnet," and "Dinosaur Air"; *The Iowa Review* online: "For the Post-Anthropocene"; *Los Angeles Review*: "Lines written on Jasper Beach, Machiasport, Maine"; *Nashville Review*: "In fear, mind"; *New Letters*: "On stillness and confluence"; *Ninth Letter*: "Lines written in the Walmart Supercenter parking lot, Lewisburg, Pennsylvania"; *Orion Magazine*: "Lines written at the tidal mudflat, Milbridge, Maine"; *Sixth Finch*: "My New Year's resolution is to become a plant"; *Smartish Pace*: "Lines written by a dairy farm, Johnson, Vermont"; *Zócalo Public Square*: "We could never stop"

"& also in that time moss draped" was inspired by many of the poems in Camille Dungy's *Trophic Cascade*, perhaps particularly by "Notes on what is always with us." "By the sidewalk I lift my child from the car" was inspired by Philip Larkin's "Sad Steps." "It's not for me but I'm here in it" was inspired by many of the poems in Ada Limón's *The Carrying*, perhaps particularly by "The Vulture & the Body." "Emergence with Periwinkle and Paint" is for M.E. Cronin and Chet'la Sebree. I am grateful to Jerry Costanzo, Cynthia Lamb, and Connie Amoroso at Carnegie Mellon University Press for their years of belief in and support for my work.

Book design by Connie Amoroso

Library of Congress Control Number 2021946599
ISBN 978-0-88748-675-3
Printed and bound in the United States of America

10 9 8 7 6 5 4 3 2 1

Contents

9   Anthropocene Lullaby

10   Lines written on Jasper Beach, Machiasport, Maine

12   I ask you, Mountain Dew bottle

13   Lines written in the Walmart Supercenter parking lot,
       Lewisburg, Pennsylvania

15   Lines written in the Down East Community Hospital
       emergency room, Machias, Maine

17   We could never stop

18   From my pocket on a hike, a tone warns me

19   Lines written on Spring Mountain trail, Mifflinburg,
       Pennsylvania, April 2020

20   I'm finefinefine & pleased

22   Lines written by a dairy farm, Johnson, Vermont

23   Still Life

24   Dinosaur Air

26   As after a hatch tadpoles heat the bank

27   Anxiety checks her phone again

29   Anthropocene Sonnet

◉

33   Lines written at the dragonfly emergence, Johnson, Vermont

35   Lines written at Dog's Head Falls, Johnson, Vermont

36   Lines written in the Rothko Room, The Phillips Collection,
       December 31, 2019

       36   *Beginning in* Green and Tangerine on Red

       38   *Beginning again in* Orange and Red on Red

       39   *Admitting in* The Ochre

       40   *Beginning again, again, in* Green and Maroon

41   Wildfires

42   My New Year's resolution is to become a plant

43   Heads with tails show up at high tide

44   I think my species needs to go or change so much it may as well have gone

45   Lines written at the tidal mudflat, Milbridge, Maine

47   Lines written at Mystic Aquarium, Connecticut

49   I write a biography of the galaxies—

50   After the dragonflies emerged, I took up the evidence

◎

53   On April 22, 2020, I remember the bodies in which I've lived

57   My child wants to go to school in the pandemic

59   Meditation on the here

61   Instead of loss, instead of grief

62   By the sidewalk I lift my child from the car

63   Walking with Zoe, holding a bag of her warm shit

64   & also in that time moss draped

65   Still Life, late October 2020

66   In fear, mind

67   On stillness and confluence

69   It's not for me but I'm here in it

71   Emergence with periwinkle and paint

72   Everything's relevant, nothing obsolete

73   After migraine, a wind pear-blooms the sidewalk

74   With all this destruction and scrambling for renewal

75   For the Post-Anthropocene

Anthropocene Lullaby

Dear Anthropocene, dear flush of spine & thumb.
The last, maybe. Last flush / flash?
A window unit hums
my swan song,
& goodbye, vertebrates.
Goodbye to us, the seas high, the sun
intensified. Anthropocene,
in the early days of spine & thumb,
was it slower? Less rise,
more cool? I ask you
for the truth.
The dead of other epochs breathe with me,
but I'm becoming all too flush
with screens, a host
of pixie-pixels—dear
Anthropocene,
still the dead flash through my face & cells,
I'm flush with them, my mind hums
with what was once their heat.
They remind me:
a lullaby repeats.

Lines written on Jasper Beach, Machiasport, Maine

A being, who was pulled out of my body nine years ago,
is building a city of stone, stick, and tangled blue string
on top of what looks like a broken cage.

Scabs and mosquito bites speckle his legs and an elbow
and he yells over the surf in his high voice,
If this one tiny twig breaks,
the whole city is going to collapse.

Something chimes, then, like a bell
warning of the end times,
but it's my iPhone. I slide its sleek body
from my pocket, scan a notification:

BREAKING NEWS.
WE JUST EXPERIENCED THE HOTTEST JUNE ON RECORD
AND IT'S PART OF A LARGER TROUBLING TREND.

I'm reading when the city shifts, sticks slumping,
stones collapsing on the cage—
which isn't only a cage, I can see now,
but a trap, built to lull and entice,

and I can almost see the insect-like shape
of all the beings who glided into it,
feeding slow in the waters, held,
before they were pulled out and boiled.

My child is squinching his forehead.
I know how to build it better, he says, dragging
toward his broken knees a red rock,
rhyolite smoothed by waves,

and balancing it on the trap, *careful,*
careful, as if he alone has been charged
with saving it all.

I ask you, Mountain Dew bottle

in the hot grass, you open-mouthed green plastic body
whose invisible cousins
swim in my gut
/ rally my cells
for transformation,
the body turned against itself,
dissolving, cascading,
when I speak
what part's plastic / what part
melded, pooled in my gut or speaking into
my brain, what part of me's melted
in the fevers in favor
of green mountains
of profit / what part
of you, plastic Mountain Dew
bottle on the hot grass
rallies in my children
from the milk of me / what part
of your mouth your voice
echoes this one I call
greenly, living, me?

Lines written in the Walmart Supercenter parking lot, Lewisburg, Pennsylvania

My child wants Pokémon cards, the most rare and evolved creatures a nine-year-old's birthday money can buy, & I want a store with no crowds, so together at 6:41 a.m., we drive Route 15 North to the Walmart Supercenter, the semis asleep in the lot, fog blurring the massive structure where something about the dawn or the fog lights up all eleven security cameras silver on the Supercenter's roof, attending like the eyes of a Madonna to a field of empty shopping carts. Inside the store, my child debates: is the Charizard EX tin better than the MewTwo EX tin, since if your health points are high but you can't do as much damage, you aren't that useful. Is it better to be able to do more damage with less health? This is unclear. But since each tin is on Clearance, the decision is moot—*both* the flying lizard & the bipedal humanoid with feline features can belong to my child, & as we sweep through self-checkout, the store's music switches on out of the silence (7:00) & the store aubades out, *Are these times contagious? I've never been this bored before. Is this the prize I've waited for?* When we walk from the fluorescent-lit body out to the body of Planet Earth, the fog has gone, & the light makes the wet lot into a mirror. The trucks still doze, but with clarity: a logging truck, a car carrier stacked with Hondas, a Dole fruit truck. Inside each truck, it occurs to me, beats a living heart, a person who'll wake the engine: a bipedal humanoid sticky from sleep, with lines pressed into the face where the pillow folded. A human whose damage-capacities and health I cannot know. I know only that the truck—the larger body to which the human tends—holds serious damage power. I climb into my car & strap my body to its larger one. I can hear from the back seat the crackle of a shrink-wrapped package opening. Eleven eyes watch us from above, eyes that could show us to ourselves: our exit from the car ten minutes ago, our entrance to the Supercenter, and our emergence with two tins depicting fantastical species now clutched by the common invasive species in the back seat—the same species serving as conductor of an entire ecological collapse—& the two of our bodies, like the bodies of the drivers of the trucks, have been swallowed into structures they did not construct, but to which they faithfully attend.

Lines written in the Down East Community Hospital emergency room, Machias, Maine

Out on the mudflats off Rays Point Road, the tide low, I stomp along-side a Muck boot-clad person who five years ago sprouted toenails in my uterus. A recent aquanaut, he peers into a tidal pool where tiny gilled creatures spin through murk. He stomps, turning back to see his prints in mud, then lifting his legs and pushing a boot into the mudshelf. He grins at how the mud sucks the boot, then slips. A tooth-sized stone bites into the meat of his knee, that just-made knee, the stone driven through deep. He screams.

At the Down East Community Hospital emergency room, a needle numbs the knee. The recent aquanaut is quiet when X-rays show the stone, a little blob with great power. Like the child. On the wall behind, a cartoon decal of an elephant smiles with gleaming teeth.

Waiting for the stone to be cut out, I switch on the TV. C-SPAN. The California Governor's Office of Emergency Services talks about trash after storms. I plug in my phone (which, having lived four years, is dying now) and let my numb-kneed child watch a video of Super Trucks.

In the last two years, four million tons of debris from disasters have been removed, says the governor's office. We're in triage, says the governor's office. Meanwhile, the elephant in the room beams at me. A giraffe decal curls her long neck around an electrical outlet.

A doctor and nurse come in. Gently, the doctor cuts out the stone. No pain. My child's knee is numb. We thank them. I change the channel, watch the U.S. Women win the World Cup.

But an animal leers at me: a lion with a full mane under the rectal thermometer. Endangered, I think. He smiles with his tongue out next to a palm tree.

My child, who shares smiles with the doctor and nurse before they go, has lived four years and will go home. But the larger body in which this four-year-old body is a blob, the larger body in which my body is a stone—that body is in triage.

We'll drive back to our rental cottage and watch the tide, which by now, five hours having passed, has hidden the flats off Rays Point Road, covered the stones, the tidewater darkening, deeper than my child's head, deeper than the heads of the mammals greater than us, the tide higher than it has yet been, and still coming in.

We could never stop

"And yet many scientists still describe geoengineering as an
inevitability—it's just so cheap, they say . . . polluting the air
on purpose to keep the planet cooler . . . and once we begin,
we could never stop."
                                —David Wallace-Wells, *The Uninhabitable Earth*

when sun falls a jellyfish this red
of aerosols the sea swims in my throat
stings of the jellyfish but not the fish
less sun less heat I'm safe except what keeps
me safe stings in the throat erects inside
the lungs protector my destroyer
from the air a killing one but safe
I'm safe the sun a jellyfish this burn
I do not come too close I breathe who's safe
until the safety keeps me from the breath
the throat falls red I sting the air my sun
what I have done what I who am this type
of thing this red erects the aerosols
to sun have done am done stings my safe air

From my pocket on a hike, a tone warns me

The end of the Paris Climate Agreement,
says my iPhone, stacking up notifications,
& meanwhile moss
mounds gentle on a boulder, moss,
green as green as greening—
a vertical happiness of spore and spread,
soft loops one to another, this
for five hundred million years,

slow to some—
time for the perceiver
isn't time for the perceived—

but neither fast nor slow to the rocks beneath me
holding their past liquid selves that swiveled
& turned, accepting,
while far off but parallel to me, a goose loiters
in an insecticide field, intoning a warning (or something else)—
which I project onto the goose to mean
I'm lost, I'm lost.
I've lost my way.

Lines written on Spring Mountain trail, Mifflinburg, Pennsylvania, April 2020

On the rocks, crust lichens cling like maps of a contagion or maps of populations. On a dead branch sweep long hatchings and cross-hatchings, insect-made maps, unreadable to me. Here fungus stains some oak turquoise in continental blobs, blue-green cup fungus, green that overlays blue, death that overlays life, one spun into the other so well they're the same weave. My children haven't gone to school in a month. This morning, the 40th day of quarantine, the younger child broke the globe on the elder's dresser. They were playing a game involving trucks, storms, and a flying Lego hero. The globe snapped from its axis and rolled off the edge of the dresser onto the hardwood floor. It's back on its axis now, but with a touch, it teeters. I use a map to walk this trail. I like the kind of map that shows curves and lines for elevation and dips, for creeks and rivers and paths that wind around the trees, showing what the land looks like in one time, stilled, as the mapmaker draws it. But even now, the earth meanders, weathers and shakes, erodes, unstill, dynamic, spewing—even now, as you read these words, as the earth pours and quakes, as "I," whoever that is to you, am not walking, and my children are not the children they were, and you, too, are not the child you were (I'm trying to include on this map, this map I'm writing, my awareness of you). And what year is it now, and how many more dead? And I wonder, in the future-to-me that is the only real thing, the present, *your* life right now, how would you map the earth in this minute, and what parts of you and your loves are even now splitting off, or shaking, or growing, and does it feel mixed up to you? Growth and death spinning? And contagion—what forms has it taken today?

I'm finefinefine & pleased

to hear the warbler who the guidebooks say
is saying *pleased to pleased to pleased to meet you,*
finefine, where a snail wends wet rocks
between boulders, its antlers testing, testing,
meeting the thisness of all this *this*
with a question—
what's safe—
& I ask it too,
spiral-shelled, moss gripping
green by the pool
[& strong-men nationalists puffbluster
inserting themselves even here] as the snail
sucks sweetness from rocks & pokes
by a pool, & that warbler, water-voiced,
says again *pleased to meetcha, fine fine fine,*
& on a woodpeckered tree, a sign:
NO TRESPASSING.
The snail sure & unsure. The snailmind
food & threat & fine,
wobbling in pebbles under water
near a pipe inserted in the bank
(what does that pipe give & take)
& the stiff grass brining water,
the vireo birching over
saying (so the guidebooks say) *here I am where are you*
here I am where are you [The strong-men nationalists
not so far from here saying *fear fear I alone will save*
you]—Dame's rocket a purple lushness

& the staghorn sumac pushing through &
here I am finefinefine, I am,
here, here, I am here.

Lines written by a dairy farm, Johnson, Vermont

Hoses coiled up by a shed. Bones
in droughted soil. Simple—how the heat

bucks in the afternoon and tractors drone
with a blue-cumulus backdrop. Not me,
but other milk-making mammals moan

nearby, packed in. Breasts bursting to be
sucked by metal pumps, sighing out sprays
of milk that if I wanted, I could drink. Not free,

but almost free. Free-ish. I guess some day
it'll change. My uncle had cows. Called them ladies.
And vice versa. These cows huddle, gray.

Why move? We can't. Don't kick. Be still. Don't see
what's right before you. Don't feel what you feel.
First, close your eyes, and then—.

Still Life

From the drainage ditch up Clay Hill Road, flies exit their eggs. A hemlock lies down to rot by a LaBatt bottle, an empty box of Natural American Spirits, & an aerosol can of dust and lint remover. A just-hatched fly patrols its side. At the top of the hill, a riding mower clips a grass rectangle around a rectangular home. A rectangular sign by the home announces a view: Awesome View! Which changes the view. Which changes any present / prior truth of the sign to a lie. Behind the hemlock: more drainage & more flies. Behind the sign: America.

Dinosaur Air

In the grocery checkout, a person called Amanda (says the nametag) snorts at a person talking too loudly on a cell. Amanda beeps through the cherries that will soon become *me*, my skin's tautness, a flow of blood. "I hate cell phones," Amanda says. I get confessional. "I'm addicted," I say. "I shouldn't have one."

"I'll never get one," Amanda says, scanning a bag of marshmallows. "I want to be *here*." Amanda gestures—not to the plastic-wrapped jet-puffed corn syrup I'm paying to make my own, but to the space between herself and me. "I want *this*." Amanda's hand waves. Me to Amanda, Amanda to me. Orbital. Drawing me back to this orbit, this turning of bodies who *feel*, real. Amanda says, confessional right back to me, "I think *this* is what I'm here for."

And the air between Amanda and me, right here in the grocery, becomes very old air. Old, old dinosaur air. Our temporary human shapes, formed of fire and prehistoric sludge, breathe the old dinosaur air. Our minds: the galaxies, before this outrageously unsustainable setup of thinkthinkthink. It's why I keep the rocks on my nightstand. And in my pockets. To remember. I'm just in *this* shape for a little time.

But it's time to give my American Express to the machine, and I do, and I watch the machine's little screen instead of Amanda, and wait for it to do its work, and the cash register spits out a paper. The thing is, I don't only keep rocks on my nightstand. I keep my cell phone there too. And in the daytime, it's in my pockets, with the rocks. "You take care," Amanda says.

"Take care," I say. I'm on my way past the vending machines, through the inner robot-doors that open for me. On the way out, my dinosaur mind, the fire and sludge mind, makes a little song, like "Amanda Cassandra, Amanda Cassandra." I check my phone for texts. The robots close the doors behind me when I exit. A key fob beeps the locks of my Subaru. I put the bag inside. I climb in and the car hums to attention. I type an address into my phone, trusting it more than I trust my own shape to know where it is I'm supposed to be.

As after a hatch tadpoles heat the bank

as after the poles heat
banks flood as after
a flooding of banks
the governments say soon
as after the saying of soon
floods unhuman the banks
/ heat floods the hatch
/ after unhumaned heat
unhatches the banks
unfloods the banked fishes
unpoles the heated poles
as after heating
who can say
soon who can say
when who becomes
what a flood afters

Anxiety checks her phone again

& each possible path through this minute glows from a screen:
two texts, a tragedy, Your Day at a Glance, breaking news.
Anxiety demands to walk not just the path she walks
but less worn paths through invisible cities

& old-growth forests, one foot in each
& a third foot on a third path through a 2,200-acre landfill
forged by anxiety herself with only a spoon.

Anxiety issues a dictum,
shames herself for not following said dictum,
shames herself for shaming herself,

sliding into the throat & ballooning,
red & blue balloons, & clowns, sad clowns,
& bakes a tasteless dry cake.

Anxiety issues just one invitation to the party,
then sighs to find one body arriving at the party,
one body that has not given enough.

Enough. One body, overrun, buzzing
with toxicity, & droughts, floods, fevers, chills,
arrives, having lost 92% of its biodiversity,
having coaxed early blooms & frozen them fruitless,
having bred mosquitoes & destroyed what was sown,
having poisoned harvests & hastened extinctions
& burnt & stormed,

having swirled with ads, warnings, poisoned harvests,
having become ad & warning & poisoned harvest,
splitting & spilling—even so,

the body arrives,
grand, multiple, & turning
this minute. A temporary miracle.

Anthropocene Sonnet

On the drive home, a busted traffic light dangles,
swinging by a wire above the snaking cars.
Furry appendages litter the road's edge, dramatizing
the entire skittery history of mammalian striving.
Born at the end of the age of sea glass, I walk
the shorelines with my eyes to my toes, bend & lift,
bend & look. I save the green, brown, & clear frosted shards
to feel with my fingers, for comfort. I set the sea glass
on my dresser with stones and shells. Meanwhile,
I play midwife to the age of sea plastics.

In the last nanosecond of the grand project of being,
I come along, make a pit stop at Baskin Robbins
to eat some sweetness, & toss away my plastic spoon—

Lines written at the dragonfly emergence, Johnson, Vermont

For seven hundred thirty nights, she scooted
and gamboled in the water's underdark.
For twenty-four full moons she burst out
to barb flesh in the water's underdark.
Then the nymph felt a largeness in her, a discomfort,
and crawled from the water onto rocks, feeling air on the skin,
and her thorax pushed her new head through,
breaking above her tubal heart a square hole,
new eyes protruding. Her legs bent, she climbed out
of herself and found footing on her cracked back,
then crouched, the abdomen dripping,
a wet expulsion, the dragonfly twice as long
as the nymph where it grew,
neither self superior, only different,

the former fine for the former world,
the present fine for the present world,
and when she spreads her new wings to dry,
the floods and heat waves she's hunkered through
show up in her wings' size, their shape,
the dragonfly body a warning of warming seas,
showing the emergency with her body in emergence,
showing need for change by her change, migrating north
beyond the range of her ancestors, to spin and gobble
and clutch in an ever-warmer earth.

Unlike the birds, who, as small reptiles
hundreds of millions of years ago,
bartered pairs of legs for wings, she insisted
on her six legs, and took wings as well,
and so became more terrifying and agile
than the angels, and more present
in the crisis, prophesying:
the only way is to transform.

Lines written at Dog's Head Falls, Johnson, Vermont

On a stone by the river   what pools in boulders
I peer into   clear on pebbles round a stick bug
who the breeze on surface film baffles & sways
gray shadow on mud ambered under
these beings   who hang suspended
head to spine to tail that twistflicks
& flips darts curls up   held to hover
over a leaf the pool's turned translucent
gold-veined   a wing an underwaterleaf—
a wing among the heads & tails—
held suspended simple   spinning
& spinning as the planet heats &
whowhat were you early   whowhat will you be?

Lines written in the Rothko Room, The Phillips Collection, December 31, 2019

Beginning in Green and Tangerine on Red

Dawn-blue over the earth's core
shook my feeling awake, the dew of it drifting
and what I'd kept burning I saw
wasn't mine but belonged to a swing
of plates, a molten interior, the holey
atmosphere. Radiance
and the melt of the poles belonged
to no one too, the night opened wide,
and what I call I was of it,
and of the heat, orange in blue,
a blue born of intensity
and set to return. Wings out
in the act of departing.
Feet to land in an arrival,
but not touching down.
I made the smog. I heated the air.
I became the smog, I slide into dormancy,
my knowing tangerined, pulp in the gut,
in the loins, and for some short sad years
what I called I was built only
to be approved, but what I was was always
a little heat, a wink,
night, stars, combustion, retraction,
pipework, subways, water flows, bodies flow,
migration. Transfer. A giving.
Such cold that heat's the same.

I gave the I itself,
planted it in the dark, let it stir in the soil,
let it subvert. A little brush fire.
The next and next. Orange was blue then.
Many eddies, foam and banter, a wave
spraying fire, a fire that rivers into a firesea.

Beginning again in Orange and Red on Red

For now the earth reds, an uncomfortable womb;
for now heat in a slaughterhouse, but not the slaughter;
for now a slow increase, so I hardly feel the boiling.

Who did I mean when I used the word *red?*
Someone near, but not me.
But I was held by red,
I was a child who sees a string hovering,
fists it tight, and rides up gently
until I slip through clouds.
I was a stain on the clouds,
and this too was fine.
A solar panel. A lump of coal.
Good only for the energy that could burst of me.
But what of the coal held by the earth?
Just there. What of the red networking of veins around an orange heart.
The heat. Comfort before the violence.
Comfort that creates violence.
An experience without expectation.
Brittle edges where a way breaks
to another way—I pass days in this tension.
Not-me sits with me,
facing the other way.
Between us, we sense in all directions.
But I don't know what not-me senses.
Me: birth, violence, heat, red.
Not-me—

Admitting in The Ochre

Really my way of living is to skulk around
sensing an opaque ochre square over everything.

I let the square hover—
all that processing of experience—
and feel the orange under it.

Feeling the orange under: not so terrible.
What sun does to a field,

softening the edge, the seeded grasses.
What crimson shoots spring from this soil?

Winds gold the fields, tornadoes whip
the horizon, clouds mull rain.

I deny nothing:
not the confusion, not the warmth,
not the marginal and not-marginal beauties

or the dusky dirt that says it's dawn.
I'm learning to admit both the orange rectangle

and the ochre square over it,
learning to say, Okay. Now.

Beginning again, again, in Green and Maroon

Even beneath the green field,
a barren plane, burnt out, parched.

Drought land.
Before and after: fires.
In the peripherals: orange.

Birth, heat, peace blueing
through a jade morning,
a fog emeralding rain, letting in
a beginning at the end,

sunrise behind the cliffs,
then a green sky granting

a green boat passage, all the seas
not yet poisoned. The before.
The after will be rich, too, the beginning

after this way of being ends.
Here is a vessel for floating.
A current. After fires, purple earth,
the early light no consciousness perceives.

Wildfires

whose home broke in heat which way holds my
hope whole whose fire's here who finds enough
red hurricane whose harm holes in my fear
no mother place please no go fire to the throat
who hurries slow I've met you when
no fear go soft whose roads sing sears
my shoes split hot a flame my fear I stir you
stir whose home falls to scatter stairs
whose stares these stares what home those screens
when strangers hold my eye the stranger broke
in burning when the sky smoked cameras spied
this night whose night whose fire you who out
has run where way enough whose home burns why

My New Year's resolution is to become a plant

& I wonder if plants sense a hermit thrush tuning eerie
through huckleberry serviceberry catberry possumhaw
holding space & twining the roots
helping

in the held space / holding the soil & I'm here & I'll hold you
/ I want to hold you huckleberry catberry possumhaw hold
until the soil goes sand

& the shrubs give to rock & the seaweed roots in intertidal flats
& in all the air I wonder

what's a barnacle to the seaweed on a shared boulder
& could it be

a holding / a helping / does one need the other
& how

to hold clear
a way of being in sun & multiple not to be named
/ labeled but holding barnacle sand crab & being held by
barnacle sand crab possumhaw catberry serviceberry—

Heads with tails show up at high tide

flick forward and seethe at the edge
of where water rubs rock, fluorescent spines & eyes
shrinking from that shadow my shadow
when I lean in to see them more & when
the current flips them their bellies flash the camouflage
of sun-on-water how the sun would look
from underneath, their sand-backs blending
with the sea-bottom & when they sense me scoot

they shockwave back as a body

& maybe they're here because the water's calm
/ maybe they hatched here / maybe too
the larger fish can't come to this drift to stalk them,
they or we who hide suspended, wiggling
under some kind of human soap-scum that violets
the surface in toxic shiver-blooms, float-cloud
that takes the shape of an origin:
an egg, a tumor, a today.

I think my species needs to go or change so much it may as well have gone

I trace a row and slide some spinach seeds
between index and thumb to wake in dirt

not dead and not alive but possibility
to multiply if they receive the drink

and soil to crack and open I can be
the soil in which to multiply a virus

invisible to me I pat the seeds
I stay away from you try not to be

the soil where the virus cracks to thrive
yet it's my kind who takes the land takes out

entire species killing them so those
that host disease can multiply the factories

that heat the sky and wake the viruses
and stir the storms I trace a row I drop

the seeds and after me the bees that brush
the clover brush the row and good I go

Lines written at the tidal mudflat, Milbridge, Maine

In this wine-water, tiny translucent creatures squinch up,
then go long. Seems that's how they get where they go,

with slight compressions and expansions of being.
Around their pool, the granite's dry. I lie on my belly, waiting

for the tide to lift the grass by the mudflat, hide the rocks,
touch my hands. Waiting for the sun to slide away.

My view says the stars slide, but they're still: I spin.
The rocks I walked on as a child seem smaller now,

but this body's grown. My mind seems to choose, but other minds
and forces guide my choice. The grass by these flats

combed out fiddler crabs riding the tide, and held them
above the flow when the tide shivered away. The seed heads

kept the crabs from sliding off and swimming back to sea.
The crabs have all dried up and died.

In time, the tide will come back in. Too late.
But maybe the crabs' story is not about separation and missed chances.

Maybe the crabs have been always a small part of the ocean, squinched up,
gone long. The best way for me to find some stars

is not by looking directly at where they should be in the sky,
but by looking elsewhere, at a spot of dark sky, my gaze averted.

That's how I seem to get where I go, or just *how* I go at all:
squinched up, then gone long, at off-angles, where I can't see the stars.

Lines written at Mystic Aquarium, Connecticut

At the aquarium's animatronic dinosaur exhibit
I spy an alligator, a real one. One eye open, golden,
spying (with no curiosity) at me:
another of the beings who puts up walls
& plastic robots that roar & turn their heads
& blink. This alligator doesn't blink,
the still eye round with force.
I meet her gaze. I know
my species built this. I worked & paid
to keep it running.
At the last mass extinction, the one that knocked out the dinosaurs,
the alligator's species slept through & crawled out live.
& then my species grew to spew out a new mass extinction
we might not sleep through—her species or mine—
& I can't say, but looking around
where kids & parents ring a fake T. rex,
I think I'd like to propose
a gift to the rest of animalia & fungi & etcetera:
shape-shifting into
the rest of the wild pulsing insistence,
losing most tools, except maybe our thumbs,
I don't know,
but I know my not knowing for sure
is part of it, necessary, because thinking I knew too much too fast
powered me here to the plastic dinosaurs
& even now the alligator's eye that I have been watching all this time
does not blink,

flecked like a galaxy viewed from beyond it
as if I broke out of my own glass, got outside
my exhibit to look from far away.

I write a biography of the galaxies—

how, once born, they spun and spread,
only in time to pull in fist-like,
pressured small, parts of them
sucking energy into a place
they could not touch but felt spiral
tight in them among the other matter,
while parts of them spat out matter
as if to fashion new, but no,
each piece they seemed to fashion
had preceded them,
and with each, more swelled
and shrank, sipped and spilled,
together shaping a whole
vaster than their added parts,
shaking on and shedding flesh, matter, energy,
some parts shrinking dense
as parts swirl and grow,
sweeping out, starred and dust-spackled,
mostly made of dark matter,
the thought of which
comforts the biographer:
dark matter holding as one a whole.

After the dragonflies emerged, I took up the evidence

When I pried a nymph skin from the rocks, the legs clung. When I lifted, they crackled. The thorax had busted open, the whiskery white tubes through which the nymph had breathed now spilled out, that defunct old system exposed. I placed three nymph skins in my pocket (as one does) and walked the mile back home. When I reached in for the skins, they'd become dust. I walked the mile back to collect more, this time carrying in my pocket an empty prescription bottle into which I placed twenty-three larval skins pulled from rocks. I saved them as a message to myself. I saved them because I felt saving larval skins would remind me not to save my own. After all, I've sat quiet and near those who migrate north towards ice that melts in cascades as they approach, and I want to remember I too am flexible, adaptive. I saved the skins because there are versions of self, shapes I wear, that no longer serve me. What emerges becomes uncomfortable, living inside an outgrown form. New ways bust through a thorax. Leave the old casing on a rock. It isn't a choice.

On April 22, 2020, I remember the bodies in which I've lived

When I lived in a young girl's body,
I held my hands in front of me
and saw what strange what stars
what shadows I could flex. But why?
Why was I not instead
a red jellyfish, or a priest?
Why this? And could some thinking be done
from the bodies of the grasses who yellowed
tall and sprouted seeds?

The bodies of the grasses, I knew,
had held the mammoths long ago,
stomping, island-fed, those last mammoths
who grazed and fought,
and nuzzled, breaths slowing for sleep,
and waking again in the shapes of mammoths.
Strangely. After so many had died.
Still, they felt the morning air in their nostrils, they yawned,
some bodies grew new mammoths, still,
as the seeds of the old grasses fell.

When I lived in a young girl's body I loved seeds,
stones, beings who like me held themselves quiet.
I was mute (selectively) and more like the grasses
than like the priests—was as sure
as the grasses, sure in their way,

which is to say
unsure, or sure only of seeming to be
another growth among the growing things.
I loved teachers, healers, those who showed
a body shelters more than one small thing.

When I had lived nearly forty years,
and wished to concentrate my feelings about being alive
in a particular shape
with a particular (and unsure and unreliable) mind,
I took an orange and halved it with a knife.
Scooped out the wet flesh, climbed in,
and lay in the half-sphere of rind and skin,
curled up like the tiny cellular-life I used to be.

I stayed. Some tried to coax me out,
but I assured them I needed to be exactly where I was.
For days, or years, I stayed in the orange skin,
and the sun baked us, the orange and I. My suffering grew.
It budded. My hope for concentrating my feelings fell away.
My fallen hope became a pollinator for the blossom,
and my love of living shrank to a single point,
like the universe before the Big Bang.
Then the orange rind spoke to me,
Once I was a pollinator in a bud, did you know? I was a bee.
Have you been a pollinator in a bud? And I said,
Rind, I have for too long been a buzzing consciousness
jostling some bud for my own purposes.

And the rind and I became
a buzz over the grass, living. We became a future:
fruit, breath, growth, expansion and contraction.

A contraction came to the last mammoths, too.
They sensed their lake shallowing, the land drying, the bodies thirsting,
the heat laughing, many slipping on the banks,
muddying the pools, and they thought,
A change is here—but still I live. Then
they didn't live. They slipped out of those shapes,
back to some more concentrated form.

My first friend was a tree, Poplar.
She held me dangling, I put my face to the circular wound
where she had lost a branch
and she fed me, she did. Sweet milk-air from between the leaves.
She was less alone than I was. She spoke, I did not speak.
She connected underground to all the other trees,
I did not connect underground to all the other selves,
or did not know, could not feel, at that time, that I did.

Now the mammoths play across some water from my sleeping,
in a blue horizon, and I wake each day in this shape, strangely,
and stay in my home, feed my young, try to keep other bodies alive.
Buds open to flowers open to fruit that contracts and drops seeds.
The mammoths hold themselves in more intense form, drawn together
in our own soft bodies, in the air we breathe.

When I lived in a young girl's body
I felt without words under attack,
and so turned to a tree, who sent secret gifts
to other trees. She sent secret gifts to me.
The tree, in sun, sent the gift of sun
to trees in shade.
As I, writing these words, send a gift to you:
the remembering that in your body, too, wake bodies,
those that attack and also those that try,
on an island in space,
in their small acts, unstilled,
not to be healed
but in the work of healing.

My child wants to go to school in the pandemic

which means wanting to go to school with his mouth
behind a piece of cloth while sitting behind plexiglass
and at a six-foot remove from other children
and risking many deaths from the viral spread
and I wonder when they do the active shooter drills

will the children crouch under desks with the lights out
spaced apart the length of a child-size coffin behind their masks
and would the newly installed plexiglass help
in the attack for which they are preparing—

my child wants to go to school
like a goose wants geese
to gather instead of migrating alone—

my child wants to go to school and learn
with other children how to crouch and cover
his head and his mouth and breathe behind a mask—

but that's not what he wants to learn,
he doesn't care about learning
as much as he cares about being
with, being with, being with, even
in the pandemic, he wants to be with—

in the actual dangerous world, not on a screen,
and I don't know what to tell him he can do,
only that when I close my eyes, I sense

how they sense each another, drawn in,
the wind less hard that way.

Meditation on the here

Here the waste treatment plant's yellow hum, here its conversions,
here particles of dust gaining particles of water, gaining heft,
gaining gray, gaining spill, which tips into giving
here inhalation, held breath, here exhalation
in the pause before the black swallowtail caterpillar crunches parsley
by the rampant basil, yellow and black and green,
then slaking off the skin and puffing into new form on a stalk,
here train horns and rumbling,
here truck static on the old highway,
here moss drying on the concrete dam,
here the creekbed rock and leaf and cracked mud,
in ten minutes as in ten hours as in ten millenia,
here the feeling it may not repeat, not this, or this,
here oil in faint curls on the low puddles that remain of creek,
here the reflection of geese gray on gray in the faint oil curl,
here a dim sun behind smoke,
here seed pods clinging to dog legs, pant legs, wool socks,
riding to where they'll grow, holding on, holding on,
then going underground,
here going underground and holding on,
here not yet opening to grow,
here burr, pod, casing, germ, cell, so many cells,
a tiny part of which
puffs up infinitely large,
here not understanding but coming into understanding,
shedding old ways, gaining new, not knowing
but understanding the scattering and unfolding
which is joy and is sorrow,

this joy, this sorrow, this joy,
this soothing, this balm, where elements play—

Instead of loss, instead of grief

Instead of loss
Instead of grief
not even or mapped
both and *and*
meltedness that sleeps
in long blue lines in mud
mate above
both cold and warmth
I carry these too
both and *and*
the *let* of things
Both *that* and *this*
a turtle's head pokes up
and at times no one but
she is and it's enough
of knowing

the Susquehanna
the mud and rocky riverbed
Instead of *instead of*
Branches melt in their tannins
waving
and striders born below
enter air
baffle and glide
Instead and
the *both and* and
the *yes and* of acceptance
and from the water
her legs paddling
a turtle knows
both her solo swim
and her warmth

By the sidewalk I lift my child from the car

What rested in his stomach seconds ago
pours out, grazes my sleeve, a fine lace of juices,
and even so my attention folds in
the car floor's blue raspberry yogurt wrappers,
fish-shaped cracker dust, the funky car-trash that sticks
along the floormat's lines;
how the goldfish, steeped in water, grow
to orange whale-size, glow golden in their bloat,
slime-puffs glistening
by translucent plastic that mirrors back sun
when I wipe my sleeve, set my child on the curb,
and meet his five-year-old brown eyes: he and I,
alive, particular, and here
in ways when I was five, and puking in a back seat,
I didn't think to think would come to be: this older
perception of what spills out
and what pours in, and doesn't pause or stop
but flows and echoes back from other years,
and changes, not all at once, but slow,
so I can barely sense it day-to-day, but do,
I do. I sense and play and work inside this change.

Walking with Zoe, holding a bag of her warm shit

my phone flashes banners, pronouncements:
the coming of sleep! Piss-pickled ice
melts into sidewalk squares. Texts burst through
the grit-laced actual, into my mind's own warm shit,
centering themselves, enchanted, affirming, whole!
My universe contracts to a glow. Cold.
Zoe tugs the leash, sniffs a snow mound—gold
with the inside sacred waters of another being.
Rooting her feet to make knowledge, real knowing
of a life: bodies eaten, pigs and pizza, stuffed chairs
and hair in muck-ice, menstrual blood,
cracked green plastic and the never-decay of a sled,
not clean stories that point toward hope and satisfy
but shard-sharp and infinite, not curations of this but *this*,
the *this* in which I had meant, way back
—and in which I mean, I do still mean—to live.

& also in that time moss draped

pale green from dead trees
and lengthened and swung
and in that time spiders swerved over
weaving nets to snare flies
and mosquitoes and yes
mosquitoes hatched and wafted over too
and sparrows and swallows with open beaks
and in that time worry danced behind quiet
and near calm sat fear and also
like the orange fungi   blooming from the dead

bloomed joy

and joy released its spores
so in that time too joy hatched
and hatched again
and those denied power defied the powerful
and storms raged and cleared for sun
and in that time inchworms lowered
their bodies on slender threads to the ground
and gathered their backs into arcs then stretched
and in that repeated act of gather and stretch
and gather and stretch   crossed distances

and thrived

Still Life, late October 2020

Not the drop-ceilinged sky shedding its wet.
Not the lance-shaped rhododendron leaves beading with green drops
but the squirrel-squawk of a warning.
And the sweet gum's green stars yellowing, soon to unstar.
Or the crow
that does not gust over, that shakes on a damp branch.
The mind unstarring. The mind a non-gust. A shake.
The mind that yellows and squawks. The mind that warns.

In fear, mind

Light bruises the cedar's eastern half,
shadow breathes the west.
Fear smacks the mind's eastern half,
joy swaddles the west.
A video game's meant-to-be-soothing tune
taunts my ears, a blue-green tune red-slapped,
like the cold that whales me when I'm hot,
rot nuzzling while I ease in sun,
swimming, chin wet,
hands scooping back water,
clearness clapping over them,
hurt hugging the joints,
the stones beneath, definite and edged,
snuggling me, burrowing in.
The stones rest, not mind or earth
but part of mind, part of earth.
When light wallops the cedar's western half
dark cradles the east. I know the lull of that,
the push and swat of knowing: easing, here.

On stillness and confluence

The wake waves wave me off elsewhere
sitting still for awhile to collide with

when the wind goes low and the leaves
nearer rattle and I hear rain soon to begin
before it begins—only when I still my own shape

and go roaming
to where a leaf flicks two particular insects

who may not be here now
but who will never not have been,
that's when I know the mind

is just the whirl or whorl a paddle sets to spin in water
to shake, a cyclone, its greatness or minuteness
only the perceiver's thought,

that swirl sliding in space by a boat's hull, front to back,
to turn turbulent for a time
and go in wider water—that's what I wish for,

which already is,
to be in this mammal shape turning
and part of, and if turning

then also turning into,
by the confluence of actions
outside and in, shaping and shaped,

distributing in wider water,
and in wider water changed.

It's not for me but I'm here in it

and when I'm trudging through tall grass to the downed tree, I trip
on an empty bottle of Two Hearted Ale,
unbroken in the onion grass and wild violets,
just by where the two-hundred-year-old oak
split-slammed and splintered into bits in a tornado,
but I'm used to tripping and falling and catching myself and getting up—
my mother always said she should have named me Grace—
so I get myself up off the ground with green-stained knees
and a white-throated sparrow whistles, *O dear, not for me,*
not for me, which I take as a sign,
maybe,
but not a sign that signifies,
and it seems this two-hundred-year-old tree
that twisted in the storm and spun to the soft earth
still blooms
this morning from its brokenness, a green-gold flowering,
even downed, with fleshy roots ripped, exposed,
and I feel a little exposed out here too, me,
and my companions skunk-scent / cut wire / pipe thing
that connects to a larger system I don't understand,
all of us, skunk-scent-cut-wire-pipe-thing-me,
not waiting, even,
all of us unreadable and not asking to be read, instead needing
to be, to be, even the split tree still in this weird fabulous-awful enterprise
of being, the soft wet moss on its bark brilliant green this morning,
fed by the storm, bright as false-hope now
when I sit down near it,
no longer walking anywhere or needing even to seem,

me and my two-heartedness,
the heart inside the body I call mine and the heart in which
the tree and I and the moss are no bigger than atoms,
and know about as much as atoms do about the whole.

Emergence with periwinkle and paint

The night I planted periwinkle roots in the dark
a friend came to my house
just to hold a penlight over me, giving me enough light
to see the hole I'd dug and the roots lowered in,
enough to see the readiness
of the soil to receive
the roots from my hands.

When the periwinkle leaves grayed and went brittle, dried out,
I trusted the secret roots, I tried to console them with water
as my friend's penlight had consoled me, to say, I'm here.
And it was true, a part of me is here still speaking to the roots,
along with whatever else was true.
Whatever else was real.

When another friend moved to a new city to work for a famous poet,
she found a new apartment, and a writing table at an antiques store
and said she wanted to paint her writing table blue,
the shade the periwinkles might become,
and I asked if I could paint it,
and she let me—because if I can't be the shape of a plant
and must be the shape I am, I want to hold the light over the soil
or the brush over the table in the hue
a friend wants the table to be.

Everything's relevant, nothing obsolete

in these low-key epiphanies I've been having—
how a potential maple tree, also called *seed*, also called *samara*,
holds other potentialities, holding a home, for instance,
for a circular cocoon, a potential moth riding a potential tree,
and I wonder which
will hatch first, plant or insect,
and will either survive, and will I
sense them, maple, moth, myself,
the collective charge of us warm with *what-is*
pressing into *what's-to-be*, an oak hurling potential oaks
also called *acorns*, sharing serendipity
for the hungry mammal who soon shows up, hello,
and nothing here—not the sticks or humid dust,
not the mask I wear or the flesh under—is outside
of relevance, nothing cast aside,
but all worthy and working for the now
and for the what soon may come.

After migraine, a wind pear-blooms the sidewalk

—confettis the curbs and ribbons of trash
and a squirrel's a furred extension of the oak
whose May skin she scrabbles, rapid sun
leaping up with the earth's spin, petalling
the stoops, jangling the bleeding
heart so it laughs, laughs wobbling red,
the ears of me open-open now like a leveled town
after wildfires, *begin again,*
the hellscape's flip-burn and plunge
undappling into clarity, hollowed out,
ready, that squirrel-oak
shaking out the leaf-fur, roots loose, *begin*
again, confettied shadows of tree-mammal
raucous-calm and ROYGBIV-ing, *begin*—what may
begin spectral—*again.* I can.

With all this destruction and scrambling for renewal

the pear tree's still swaddled
by its petals, clouds pooling over,

and this is the pear tree I watched
a dump truck back into last May, split off

the largest bough, dangling when the chain saws
screamed in to finish the job—

with or without the human, with or without the vertebrates
dying off, life wills itself more life

and I breathe in exhaust & pollen,
sneezing out both, what I call *me*

another growing thing, an arrangement of cells,
wildness as it will be, as it has been.

For the Post-Anthropocene

—at Roque Bluffs state park
stone stone & skipping barefoot tender
on stone sand & heat / sharpness or roundness guiding
to go on wanderlooking
but not looking for
no not to find but what's now found & now, seeing
I see
& if I bend to touch a rock to palm
a rock the wind wobbletosses a force
I'll be too, a little bluff wind a rough rogue
the stones too I'll be so I could
point the body now to serve the larger body
in which my body's just a cell
/ something working in the cell,
to join
like a little bluff wind (aware)
/ serve the whole
so other bodies may go on
to see stone & skip tender—

A May 2018 fellowship at Vermont Studio Center and the friends I met there helped this book to begin; thanks to Brenda Peynado, Josh Aiken, Sarah Green, VV Ganeshananthan, Sonya Larson, Danit Brown, Andrea Martin, Jody Gladding, and others. Likewise, sojourns at Pendle Hill between 2016 and 2019 allowed me to work on this book while in community with Friends and other sojourners. I'm grateful to my parents, Camilla Tassone Hays and Robert Hays, and to my spouse, Andrew Ciotola, for the many ways they gave me time and space to myself while I wrote and revised these poems. To Peg Cronin and Chet'la Sebree: thank you for seeing me and believing in these poems during the seven years I worked on them, and for the bright influence of your own writing. To Arlo and Leo Ciotola: thank you for your being, now and in every now to come. To Andrew Ciotola: I'm more grateful than I can say for your devotion to the arts, to the woods, and to the good braiding of our lives. I thank my colleagues at Bucknell University, especially those in the Creative Writing Program and English Department, for their support and inspiration. Special acknowledgement and deep gratitude to Shara McCallum, Jan Verberkmoes, and Todd Davis, for sharing suggestions for and responses to this manuscript as it took shape, and helping it to reach its final form. I'm also grateful for the undergraduates who have joined me for workshops, for the always-luminous Karen Bald Mapes (1957-2013), for every one of the Junies, and for Erica DelSandro, Celia Shiffer, Tasha Hall, Carolina Ebeid, Betsy Wheeler, Jane Hirshfield, Juanita and Barry Bishop, Karen Frock, Iris and Robert Gainer, Nancy Robinson, Molly Brown, Christopher Camuto, Analicia Sotelo, Danielle Deulen, Donika Kelly, Aurora Masum-Javed, Mary Ruefle, Ada Limón, Camille Dungy, Mukta Phatak, Aracelis Girmay, Mary Szybist, Marjorie Maddox, Diana Khoi Nguyen, Shane McCrae, Julia Kasdorf, Robert Rosenberg, Leslie Sainz, Chinelo Okparanta, Andrea Deibler-Gorman, Raena Shirali, EG Asher, Martha Park, Rachel Sussman, Shara Lessley, Mary Jo Bang, Carl Phillips, Simonne Roy, Deirdre O'Connor, Arlyne Hoyt, Joseph Scapellato, Laure Rohrs Gargano, Sara Chuirazzi, Jackson Pierce, Tara Kemp, Ann Keeler Evans, Angèle Kingué, Kimi Cunningham Grant, and Paula Closson Buck: for your work, which influences mine, and for your light.